TO CALL A MUTT COOL IS REDUNDANT. ALL MUTTS ARE

COOL BY DEFINITION. THEY'RE HEALTHIER THAN FANCY

PUPPY-MILL DOGS. THEY'RE NOT SURLY AND SELDOM

SUFFER FROM CHRONIC MELANCHOLIA. LIVING ON THE

EDGE HAS ENDOWED THEM WITH A KEEN SENSE OF

SURVIVAL AND AN INGRAINED SENSE OF LOYALTY.

AND BEST OF ALL, THEY'RE ALMOST ALWAYS FREE.

J. C. SUARÈS

SUSAN EVANS BOHAN
MANHATTAN BEACH, CA, JUNE 1996
"Sasha, my two-and-a-half-year-old German
shepherd-retriever-border collie mix loves it when I
speak to her in double-vowel words. I say, 'Would
you like some food or a cookie or how about Shamu
(which she thinks is Shamoo).' She sits and cocks
her head whenever I talk this way to her."

COOL

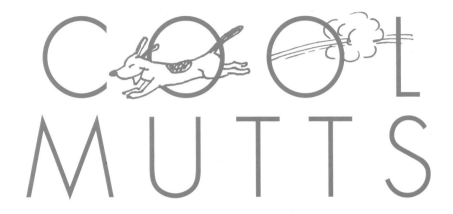

MUTTS

EDITED BY

J. C. SUARÈS

TEXT BY

H. D. R. CAMPBELL

PHOTO RESEARCH BY

KATRINA FRIED

WELCOME ENTERPRISES, INC.

NEW YORK

First published in 1997 by
Welcome Enterprises, Inc.
New York

Distributed by Stewart, Tabori & Chang, Inc.
a division of U.S. Media Holdings, Inc.
115 West 18th Street, New York, NY 10011
Distributed in Canada by General Publishing Co., Ltd.
30 Lesmill Road, Don Mills, Ontario, Canada M3B 2T6
Distributed in the U.K. by Hi Marketing
38 Carver Road, London SE24 9LT, United Kingdom
Distributed in Australia and New Zealand by Peribo Pty. Limited
58 Beaumont Road, Mount Kuring-gai NSW 2080, Australia

Library of Congress Card Catalog Number: 97-060492
ISBN 1-55670-681-2

Printed and bound in Italy
10 9 8 7 6 5 4 3 2 1

She was just sitting there on the sidewalk, looking up at me. Our eyes met, and when they did I felt a physical jolt, like a connection being made. A spark leaped between us as though there were electrical wires leading from her to me. I wasn't able to take my eyes off her face; I could swear she smiled at me.

That dog had the most appealing face I'd ever seen, bright and intelligent and curious and sweet, all at the same time. And something else shone from her face, something I had no words for then, but would come to know as deep wisdom, enormous kindness, and generosity of spirit. She was truly spiritual. Under her fluffy white eyebrows she had a pair of eyes that would melt a rock, eyes that were sympathetic, merry, and knowing. Just one look is all it took. You're going to be my dog, I thought.

PHILIP GONZALEZ AND LEONORE FLEISCHER
THE DOG WHO RESCUES CATS: THE TRUE STORY OF GINNY

TITLE PAGE:
ELLIOTT ERWITT
CENTRAL PARK, NEW YORK, NY, 1977
Sandy, star of the Broadway musical *Annie,*
takes a break in Central Park with his owner.

Blackie, Brownie, Whitey, Frosty, Snowflake, Spot: Mutts. Unlike fancy breeds, mutts don't need fancy names or expensive grooming. They're the most loyal dogs, and most of the time they're free for the taking. Often taken for granted and sometimes abandoned, they don't always have the easiest of lives. Yet under every scruffy exterior beats the heart of a potential best friend.

Until I met Warren, I never understood people's attraction to mutts. He was a German shepherd-beagle mix who lived in Pennsylvania, where I have a weekend house. Warren had once belonged to a couple who abused and abandoned him. As a result, he was terrified of strangers and had a growl that scared everyone away. But Warren was a social creature underneath it all, and after awhile he befriended some neighbors who lived next to the field where he lived with a local farmer's cows.

When I met him, they said, "Don't be afraid, he is just scared of you. He'll smell you and never forget you." I stood still and tried not to be afraid as Warren paced around me, sniffing and growling. The next time I went to visit, Warren ran toward me barking. I tried to tell him we already knew each other. I put my hand out. He smelled it and kept barking but let me pass. This kind of greeting continued for weeks as I hoped that Warren would eventually learn that not all humans meant him harm. Many months later, he relaxed a bit and allowed me to tentatively pet the top of his head. It felt to me as if something wonderful were happening.

For a long time Warren remained an outside dog. He lived with cows all week long and only came to the house for food, which he would only eat if it were placed outside. My friends bought him a red dog house for Christmas and installed it on the porch, and Warren soon began to spend weekends there. In time, I could pet him and he could be coaxed inside the big house. When my friends were away on weekends, I would go over to feed him. I would call him, and after a few minutes he would come running up the two-lane road. We were getting to know each other better though I could tell he was a little bit wary.

One night when I was at our friends' house for dinner, Warren, who had come inside, lay down on my feet under the dinner table. That was it. I finally got it.

It was so simple: It was love. Warren cared for me. He was content just to be near me. I bent down and gave him a big hug. He acted like it was the most natural thing in the world. Now I know how special Blackie, Brownie, Whitey, Frosty, Snowflake, and Spot all are and why. And though I missed out on having a mutt of my own when I was a little girl, I have a friend in Warren who more than makes up for it now.

H. D. R. Campbell

I like a bit of a mongrel

myself, whether it's a man or

a dog; they're best for every day.

GEORGE BERNARD SHAW

JANE LIDZ
EUGENE, OR, 1976
Zak, the bathtub martyr. The expression
on his face illustrates exactly how he
feels about getting a bath.

ULNIKA ÅLING
STOCKHOLM, 1994

"I was taking pictures of people in a newly built
section of Stockholm. I put a mask on each person to
make him or her more anonymous. Then the dog
turned up and he too wanted to be photographed
and joined in the spirit of the moment."

ABOVE:

YLLA

NEW YORK, NY, PRE-1945

This sweet yawning puppy became
famous after the Humane Society
hung this picture in its offices.

OVERLEAF:

ABIGAIL J. HODES

NEW YORK, NY, 1995

"One day while riding the New York City
subway, I looked down and spotted this experienced
little rider calmly waiting for his stop."

Dogs love company. They

place it first in their

short list of needs.

J. R. ACKERLEY

PHOTOGRAPHER UNKNOWN
ABOARD SHIP, OCTOBER 29, 1943

Picked up by a member of the crew of a Navy transport, Mr. Chips found himself a member of Uncle Sam's Navy before he could wag his tail and bark assent. Smuggled aboard ship by his master, Chips instantly became the mascot of the whole crew. Discovered and ordered ashore by the executive officer, Chips was "rescued" by his new-found friends whose pleas softened the exec's heart. Since then Chips has become literally an old sea dog. He participated in the grim business of the attack on Attu. When the Kiska venture began, Chips perhaps sensed the enemy had left and remained aboard ship. Like every other member of the Navy, Chips has a health record, an identification card and, of course, a dog tag.

(Original caption, circa 1943)

Don't make the mistake

of treating your dogs like

humans, or they'll treat

you like dogs.

MARTHA SCOTT
Dogs

MARILAIDE GHIGLIANO
ROME, ITALY, 1990
"One day at a busy intersection at the Piazza Venezia in front
of the Vittorio Emanuele II monument, I saw two tourists with this
darling little puppy. I think they may have rescued him because
they were well-dressed while he had no collar or tag, only a mere
cord around his neck. They didn't notice me on the ground taking
pictures between their legs. If someone had photographed me at that
moment, who knows what they would have thought I was doing."

ABOVE:

PELLE WICHMANN

FARO, SWEDEN, 1978

"I took this picture while I was bicycling around the island of Faro in the Baltic Sea where Ingmar Bergman lives. I met this boy and dog when I passed some houses near the sea. The dog belonged to the boy's grandfather whom the boy was visiting for the summer. The old, fat dog who could not move easily and the thin, young boy who was quite nimble appeared to be very good friends."

RIGHT:

PHOTOGRAPHER UNKNOWN

HOLLYWOOD, CA, 1920s

The Little Rascals from the *Our Gang* comedy film series included Pete, the Pup, a pit bull mix, complete with his movie makeup, a freshly drawn circle ringing his right eye.

OVERLEAF:

THOMAS WESTER

SMÅLAND, SWEDEN, 1986

A dog and his master relax on a hot summer day with their friends.

MARILAIDE GHIGLIANO
LANGHE, ITALY, 1992

"This mutt lives in an isolated farmhouse in the hills of Langhe near Mondovi. He is a truffle hunter. I went there to photograph the barn animals, but the dog attracted my attention because he wanted the loaf of bread that I had for the pigs. He ate all of it. According to the farmer, the dog had never been interested in bread before; he was just trying to get his picture taken!"

RIGHT:

MARILAIDE GHIGLIANO
LANGHE, ITALY, 1993

"This dog lived in Lovera, a tiny village hidden in the hills of Langhe near Dogliani. He was chewing his bone in the town square in front of an inn. As I stopped to photograph him, another dog came near. He assumed the dog wanted his bone. But the dog just waited for him to finish his bone and then they went for a long walk together in the hills."

OVERLEAF:

PHOTOGRAPHER UNKNOWN
PLACE UNKNOWN, DATE UNKNOWN

The dog who bit off more than he could chew.

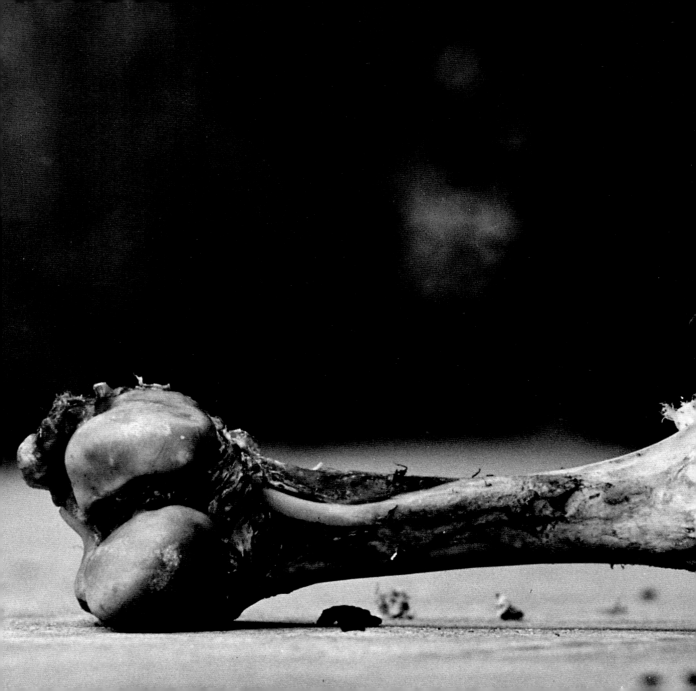

When the Man waked up he said,

"What is Wild Dog doing here?"

And the Woman said,

"His name is not Wild Dog any

more but the First Friend,

because he will be our friend

for always and always and always.

RUDYARD KIPLING

MARILAIDE GHIGLIANO
CASTIGLIA DEL NORD, SPAIN, 1985
"I was in the town of Moarves to photograph a beautiful
Romanesque church. At one point I heard barking and turned
to see this puppy peeking out of the beaded curtains of the bar
near the church. While I photographed him he darted in and
out of the curtains, turning our meeting into a game."

THOMAS WESTER
STOCKHOLM, SWEDEN, 1988

"This boy and his dog were playing
in a schoolyard. The dog hung onto
the rope and the boy swung him
around and around. They played
this way until finally both staggered
away like two drunken sailors."

PHOTOGRAPHER UNKNOWN
MOSCOW, RUSSIA
JANUARY 15, 1989

A dog desperately tries to pull
a baby carriage on the icy ground
outside the main entrance to
Novodevichy Convent in Moscow.

Dogs love their friends and bite their
enemies, quite unlike people, who are
incapable of pure love and always have
to mix love and hate in their object relations.

SIGMUND FREUD

MARILAIDE GHIGLIANO
BRITTANY, FRANCE, 1990

This dog happily viewed the Fête de Filets Bleus
(which takes place every August in Concarneau)
from its master's backpack.

RIGHT:

ROBIN SCHWARTZ
PARAMUS, NJ, 1995

Ginger poses in her pumpkin outfit at the Halloween
costume contest held annually at the Pet Nosh super store.

I believe that dogs are very capable of applying

their minds in an array of situations. And the

degree of their intelligence can vary from breed

to breed and dog to dog—just like people.

WARREN ECKSTEIN WITH ANDREA ECKSTEIN
How To Get Your Dog To Do What You Want

JOHN DRYSDALE
OUNDLE, ENGLAND, 1981

Mr. Magoo, the pet of an elephant trainer in Oundle, England,
loved to go mountaineering on Maureen, a three-ton elephant with
a tolerant nature. Magoo, a poodle-pinscher mutt and six months
old in this photograph, would make the perilous ascent up the
elephant's leg. Then Maureen would raise her leg, enabling Magoo to
scamper onto her shoulder and continue onto her trunk. Maureen
curled her trunk around the tiny pup as the finale to this circus trick.

RIGHT:

RIGHT:
MARC RIBOUD
PARIS, FRANCE, 1953

Proving the extreme lengths to which canines will go to please
their master, two incredibly brave and agile dogs
perform on tightropes in an outdoor street circus in Paris.

OVERLEAF LEFT:
JOHN DRYSDALE
LONDON, ENGLAND, 1990

"This dog belonged to the operator of the roundabout. At first
she rode the swings on her master's lap. Later, having become
an 'expert,' she jumped on the swings at will. Her master
perched the tiny cap on her head to amuse his patrons."

OVERLEAF RIGHT:
JOHN DRYSDALE
LONDON, ENGLAND, 1990

A fox terrier crossed with a wire-haired terrier (and others)
earns his keep in a London street circus. The little dog's owner
passes the hat while keeping an eye out for the local police.

JOHN DRYSDALE
RUTLAND, ENGLAND, 1984

"Whenever her owner went waterskiing, Merry, a collie-labrador
mutt, would swim out to her mistress and tow her skis back in her
mouth. On successive ski runs, she would try to climb aboard too.
Later on a board especially adapted for her, she got her wish to
ski and would bark and wag her tail enthusiastically during the
whole ride. Then she took to riding on her owner's skis and grew
to prefer waterskiing to walking in the summertime."

A motorcycling mutt with his own small
helmet and goggles takes to the road.

If you pick up a starving dog and make him

prosperous, he will not bite you. This is the

principal difference between a dog and a man.

MARK TWAIN

PELLE WICHMANN
PARIS, FRANCE, 1980
"I was strolling around Montmartre in Paris off-season
and suddenly a little black dog came walking toward
me. He stopped outside the bakery. He seemed to
know it well; he sniffed and wagged his tail very fast.
I think the dog knew the owner of the shop."

ROBIN SCHWARTZ
CENTRAL PARK, NEW YORK, NY, 1993

In Central Park, dogs are not supposed to be allowed off their leashes, but they are released and sent for swims anyway. People throw sticks and they jump right in. This is a very common sight.

RIGHT:
TONY MENDOZA
GRAYTON BEACH, FL, 1990

A mutt poses for a photography project called *Dogs On Vacation*.

OVERLEAF:
ABIGAIL J. HODES
DINGLE PENINSULA, IRELAND, 1996

This canine sentry pops out of the building and alerts his master when tourists arrive at the gate to his property. His master then charges the tourists a small fee to cross the field leading to the local ruins.

A very casual and unconcerned basset hound mix
snoozes on the sidewalk as people walk around him.

I'd rather have an inch of dog

than miles of pedigree.

DANA BURNET
MUTTS

JOHN DRYSDALE
LONDON, ENGLAND, 1955
"On a London street closed to traffic, this mutt was
engrossed in a football game with a small group of
boys who treated him as an equal player. When I took
this picture, the dog was acting as goalkeeper. He was
so skilled, none of the boys managed to score."

DONNA RUSKIN
PURCHASE, NY, 1980

"I was working in the photography department at
SUNY. One day on my way to work, I saw this dog tied
up outside. He was very vulnerable and sweet-looking.
After I took this picture, I never saw him again."

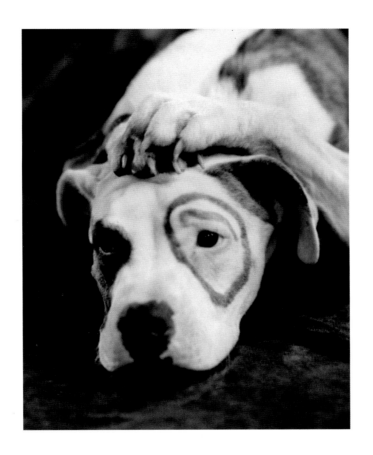

PHOTOGRAPHER UNKNOWN
HOLLYWOOD, CA, 1920s

Pete the Pup, a star in his own right,
poses for this close-up publicity shot
for the *Our Gang* comedy film series.

This dog is going to learn your every desire. He'll learn to work from heel and retrieve on command whether it be land or water. He'll learn to follow your whistle and hand signals. He'll learn when to do the retrieving job on his own and when to depend on you. I think the bond between dog and man is stronger in the retriever breeds than in any of the other hunting dogs because of the basic requirement of the teamwork necessary to get the job done.

RICHARD A. WOLTERS
WATER DOG

RIGHT:
TONY MENDOZA
GRAYTON BEACH, FL, 1990
A classic combination, a dog and his ball
photographed in the surf at Grayton Beach, Florida,
for a photography project called *Dogs On Vacation*.

RIGHT:

ANTONÍN MALÝ

PRAGUE, CZECH REPUBLIC, 1989

"I took this picture of my eldest daughter,
Helene, and my older dog, Eman, one day
after the Velvet Revolution in Prague."

OVERLEAF:

ANTONÍN MALÝ

SKALICE, SOUTHERN BOHEMIA, 1995

The photographer's dogs, Eman and
Bilbo, playing near their weekend house.

64

Sandy (on counter), the star of the musical *Annie,* and
her understudy in their dressing room at the theater.

When I was a kid, maybe nine or ten years old, I was walking with some of my friends on the beach, and we saw a pack of homeless dogs. They weren't vicious, just playful, but while we were watching them, the dogcatcher's van pulled up, and the dogcatcher went after them. He nabbed a few of them and shoved them into the back of his van. Then he took off after the others. As soon as he was out of sight, my pals and I went to work. We got the back of the van open, and all the dogs spilled out and ran away—not only the beach dogs, but others he had rounded up too. We didn't do it to be mischievous; we did it to help the jailed dogs.

PHILIP GONZALEZ AND LEONORE FLEISCHER
THE DOG WHO RESCUES CATS:
THE TRUE STORY OF GINNY

KURT HUTTON
ASCOT, ENGLAND, 1949
The Stevenson family has been training circus dogs for three generations. In their winter quarters at Ascot, Asta, who is part terrier, stays in shape by jumping over the vacuum cleaner.

BÖRJE TOBIASSON
NAPLES, ITALY, 1986

A pack of street dogs out on
their morning rounds.

One of a series of photos called *The Leila Pictures*. In
Hebrew, *leila* means "night"; a perfect name for this mutt.

ROBIN SCHWARTZ
HOBOKEN, NJ, 1995

Someone brought Copper from Pueblo, Mexico. Now
he lives with a family in a house with a backyard.

DEAN
PLACE UNKNOWN, DATE UNKNOWN
Let sleeping dogs lie...

The best thing about a man is his dog.

PROVERB

WALTER CHANDOHA
WEST HAMPTON, NY, 1959
"I met this mutt on the beach.
I petted him and he licked my hand."

PHOTO CREDITS

Cover, 10: Ulnika Åling
Backcover, 49, 63, 74: Tony Mendoza
1: Susan Evans Bohan
2, 35, 53, 69: © Elliott Erwitt/Magnum Photos
7: Leo Huffman
9: Jane Lidz from Zak: *The One of a Kind Dog*,
  published by Harry N. Abrams ©1997
11: Ylla
12–13, 50–51: Abigail J. Hodes
15, 19, 57: Courtesy Culver Pictures
17, 22–23, 27, 36: Marilaide Ghigliano
18, 47: Pelle Wichmann
20–21, 30–31: Thomas Wester
24–25, 32–33: Courtesy Corbis-Bettman
28–29, 45, 71: Courtesy Hulton Getty
37, 48, 75: © Robin Schwartz,
  courtesy Sarah Morthlande Gallery, NYC
39, 42–44, 55: © John Drysdale
41: Marc Riboud/Magnum Photos
56, 59: Donna Ruskin
60–61: Mary Bloom
65–67: Antonín Maly
72–73: Börje Tobiasson
77: Courtesy Archive Photos
79: Walter Chandoha

Text: H.D.R. Campbell
Drawings: J.C. Suarès
Photo Research: Katrina Fried
Design: Tania Garcia